ALMOST DONE WRITING:
NOW WHAT?

A GUIDED WORKBOOK *for* **SELF-PUBLISHING AUTHORS**

Foreword by Diane Riis

ANDREA SCHMIDT

A-SCHMIDT MEDIA

ALMOST DONE WRITING: NOW WHAT?
A GUIDED WORKBOOK *for* **SELF-PUBLISHING AUTHORS** (NONFICTION)
Copyright © 2021 Andrea Schmidt (A-Schmidt Media)

All rights reserved. No part of this book may be reproduced in any form without permission in writing from the publisher, except by a reviewer who may quote brief passages in a review. Every effort has been made to include accurate, current information. However, if you find an error feel free to report it at **ANDREA@BOOKDESIGNER.CA**. *The author assumes no responsibility for errors, inaccuracies or omissions, and hereby disclaims any liability to any party for any loss, damage, or disruption caused by errors or omissions, whether such errors or omissions result from negligence, accident, or any other cause.*

CREDITS
Book cover and interior design by Andrea Schmidt *(a-schmidt.com)*
Copyediting by Jenny Watz *(writeambitions.com)*

DO YOU NEED A BOOK DESIGNER?
If you are seeking an experienced book designer for your nonfiction book project, visit **BOOKDESIGNER.CA**

978-1-9992724-0-1 (PAPERBACK)
978-1-9992724-7-0 (EBOOK)

First Edition

Printing and distribution: worldwide POD via IngramSpark/KDP

PLEASE LEAVE AN HONEST REVIEW for this book:
1) Login to the site where it was purchased
2) Find the "Write a Customer Review" button

Thank you!

♥ **THIS BOOK IS DEDICATED TO YOU** *for* **BRINGING YOUR CREATIVITY** & **WISDOM INTO THE WORLD FOR THE BENEFIT OF OTHERS**

CONTENTS

4	FOREWORD
5	INTRODUCTION
6	EDITING
6	The **BIG PICTURE:** Timeline
7	**TA-DA!** Imagining An Amazing Outcome
9	**BOOK SALES & MARKETING** (Intro)
11	Finding **THE PERFECT BOOK TITLE**
19	**BOOK COVER RESEARCH:** Your Homework
23	Receiving **BOOK COVER MOCKUPS**
25	Creating **A BOOK LAUNCH SUPPORT TEAM (BLAST)**
31	**INTERIOR** Book Design & **FORMATTING**
37	Some **EYE-WATERINGLY BORING** Stuff!
41	**FRONT & BACK BOOK MATTER**
43	**ADVANCE REVIEWS:** Getting Social Proof
51	**PROMOTIONAL COPY**
55	The **BACK COVER & SPINE**
57	**THINKING AHEAD TO YOUR BOOK LAUNCH**
63	Generating Excitement: **YOUR PRE-LAUNCH CAMPAIGN**
77	Ordering **PRINTED BOOKS**
81	**BOOK SALES & MARKETING:** Make a Plan!
90	**CHECKLIST:** Is My Book Ready for Publishing?
91	Hitting **"PUBLISH"**

PLANNING TOOLS

	93	Calendar: **1 YEAR**
	94	Calendar: **5 MONTHS**
	104	**SWIPE FILE**
	105	Your **PASSWORDS**
	107	**EDITORS & BOOK COACHES**
109	Acknowledgments	
109	About the Author	
110	Glue **A PICTURE OF YOURSELF HERE HOLDING A BOOK**	

FOREWORD

When I first met Andrea Schmidt I had been editing and coaching authors for five years. I found that as my authors were finishing their books, instead of celebrating, they were mired in "what next?" questions that I just didn't know how to answer. I was releasing them into the wilds of book design, copyediting and marketing without a guide.

My writers needed mindset, writing and editing help, yes, I can handle that, but they needed more. I created Earth and Soul Coaching and Publishing for this very reason. To be a guiding hand for authors who want help every step of the self-publishing way.

But who could I hand my precious writers off to? Well, Andrea Schmidt and I connected, and during the course of a conversation that extended over one long, lovely spring afternoon, I knew I had my answer. I had a referral partner I would come to love and trust.

Today I introduce Andrea to clients, knowing she is a woman with soul, creativity, generosity and gentleness. She will be kind. Professionally she is tops, with a real understanding of what a cover should do to represent and market a book. She is an expert in the wild, wild west of self-publishing. Any Facebook group will tell you to design your own book with tools you can download for free. I beg you not to do that and it invest in a skilled, seasoned, smart designer. Someone who understands the process and stays on the cutting edge of new developments. Like Andrea Schmidt.

While anyone with a manuscript and a dream can upload a book to Amazon, in order for the book to look and feel professional and have the result an author craves, it needs an expert eye and skill. Andrea is that expert. From folks who've never published before to those who believe they've already got this publishing thing all figured out, I recommend you speak to the expert.

My two favourite words for clients wondering whether their title, cover, or visibility idea is any good are: "Ask Andrea."

Since then, I've worked with her to guide people in a way that is smart, efficient, and attentive to the client's unique situation. In this workbook you will hear her voice and if you're smart, you'll let it guide you to the solutions you need to simply, competently and thoroughly handle wherever you're at in the process of writing your nonfiction book.

Most recently, a client of mine held up this workbook during a Zoom call and said, "This is beautiful and so simple! I will do everything it says, one step at a time. I was overwhelmed and thought this was going to be just another thing to do. But, it will actually make everything easier."

So, rather than go off into the wilds of self-publishing all by yourself, use this book and save yourself the heartache of trying to figure it out alone. And when you want to really get out of the woods, ask Andrea to be your guide.

—Diane Riis, writer's coach and author of *Sh*t: How a Four Letter Word Can Change Your Life (Transforming Your Story from Inside Out)* and the upcoming: *Your Words are Magic,* a how-to for women who want to get unstuck and heal their writer's block for good

INTRODUCTION

Seemingly endless hours of writing and editing and re-writing and more re-writing and more editing, proofreading and more revisions are slowly coming to a close. You are wondering… What now?

To paraphrase Mr. Nelson Mandela, my most simple answer to this question is: **CELEBRATE**. *I highly recommend that as you progress through this journey (learning and sometimes fumbling as you go), take time to celebrate along the way!*

My name is Andrea Schmidt and I am proud of you, and excited about how far you have come. As a chronic "starter" of projects, I understand how much time, energy, and commitment goes into writing a book – and finishing it!

Last fall I was gardening in my front yard when I accidentally banged a wasp's nest with my shovel. Swarmed from all angles, I ran around shrieking in confusion as the yellow jackets latched on to my clothes, biting and stinging me in multiple places.

Wildly, I managed to swat them away and retreat back to the safety of my house so I could reassure my bewildered daughter (and myself) that I was going to survive.

Let's be honest: for many authors, the thought of launching a book may be worse than unexpectedly getting swarmed by wasps. When you consider the idea, you may experience dread. You may feel queasy. Your mind may swarm with feelings of discomfort about your social media presence and how to build an "author platform."

Those feelings are normal for authors. Writing a book is a lot of work, but launching a book brings up issues of vulnerability. Those feelings are like yellow jackets, and we need to find a way to work with them.

If you've done any amount of preliminary research, you may feel as though self-publishing is confusing as heck! The self-publishing road is strewn with conflicting advice, depending on (for example) the point of view of the advice-giver, and what year that blog post was published. There is no one clear simple path for self-publishing.

But here's the truth: if you really didn't want to share your book with others, you would keep it hidden in your desk drawer. Since you are planning to release it, it's time to come out of hiding.

Since you've come this far: there will be a book. And hence, there will be some kind of "launch." Since you have gone to the trouble of writing the book and working with an editor (or multiple editors) and you are planning to publish your book into the world, you are actually more ready than you know to tackle the next task of getting your book out there. Sharing your wisdom and stories.

You are ready to shine. Or, if not quite "ready to shine," then you are ready to not hide in a cave. You will not do this alone.

Imagine how great you will feel afterward, knowing that not only did you write a great book, but that you also put your best foot forward to share it with the people who will most benefit from and enjoy it!

My highest hope with this guided workbook is that it will help you a) transform your manuscript into a highly professional book, b) prioritize your book marketing activities, c) soothe you when you feel despair, and d) share your writing with the people who will most benefit from it – in a way that feels authentic to you.

–*Andrea Schmidt*

EDITING/PROOFREADING

This workbook assumes you've already had your book edited (and possibly proofread as well). If you still need to find an editor to help you on your self-publishing journey, feel free to seek out any of the incredible, talented editors and book coaches listed on page 107.

If your writing has stalled, you are feeling stuck, and you want help, contact Diane Riis (earthandsoulpublishing@gmail.com) who runs "high vibe writing" sessions and retreats.

TIP: Learning to "self-edit" your own writing is a valuable skill for an author.

THE BIG PICTURE: TIMELINE

Having a rough book launch date in mind as you move forward will help you organize and work backwards with the many "to-do" tasks on your list. When considering your launch date, keep in mind that book production and launch planning can easily take between four and six months (or more). Rushing inevitably leads to mistakes.

Lately, a lot of my clients are choosing their birthday as their launch date. Great! Or do you have a big speaking gig coming up that you can synchronize with your launch? Or perhaps November/December, when people are in the mood to spend money? September is a traditional time to launch a book, so there are often quite a few books coming out then.

TIP: If this feels stressful, just come back to it later.

Here's an example of what a rough book launch timeline could look like:

MARCH: Working on the title/subtitle

APRIL: Proofreading/revisions, book design, thinking about your pre-launch campaign

MAY: Sending out Advance Review Copy PDFs in order to get advance reviews (and catching typos!)

JUNE: Finalizing the book's back cover and interior

JULY: Pre-launch and launch planning, fine-tuning the marketing plan

AUGUST: Taking a breather! Implementing your marketing plan, stress-free

SEPTEMBER: Uploading your files, launch

ONGOING: Book marketing activities

TIP: *Selling books* usually turns out to be more challenging than most people expect. For this reason, book marketing experts suggest thinking about your target audience (see page 63) and marketing plan (page 81) as early as possible, ideally even before you write the book. Personally, I also like to build lots of extra "breathing room" into my schedule before launching in order to focus completely on my marketing ideas without too much pressure. Why stress yourself unnecessarily?

If it's helpful for planning, use the calendar pages at the back of this workbook (see page 93) .

MY BOOK LAUNCH DATE: _____

TA-DA! YOUR BOOK
IMAGINING AN AMAZING OUTCOME

You are doing something amazing: creating a wonderful book that only you could write. *Congratulations!*

As if that weren't enough, you're bravely planning to share it with people who will enjoy, learn from, and benefit from it.

You may be terrified! Excited! Scared and confused. But here's the thing: you don't need to know all the steps that are yet to come. *Just keep moving forward!*

STATEMENT OF ENCOURAGEMENT
E.g., "I am proud of myself for creating a book that will help people!" "I love myself. I trust myself."

> **RETURN TO THIS PAGE TO ENCOURAGE YOURSELF IF/WHEN YOU FEEL FEAR OR DOUBT**

STATEMENT OF COMMITMENT
E.g., "I commit to finishing this book and launching it to the best of my ability."

NOTES:

BOOK SALES & MARKETING
INTRO

Most of the work we do in this workbook relates to book sales and marketing in one way or another.

First we write the best book we possibly can, and have it edited and proofread so it's the best it can be. Then we transform and design it into a gorgeous product, tailored to benefit a specific reader.

Then, ultimately, it falls on us independent authors to help our readers find and connect with it. Everything we'll be doing here supports that goal:

- Identifying your audience (page 63)
- Making sure your book title and cover are professional and compelling to your readers
- Proactively gathering social proof for your book
- Uploading your book to one or more self-publishing platforms
- Planning a pre-launch campaign to generate excitement for your book
- Planning a book launch
- Creating a marketing plan and selling your book

JUMP TO PAGE 81 AND START DREAMING UP ALL THE INTERESTING WAYS YOU WILL SHARE YOUR BOOK WITH PEOPLE!

As soon as you feel ready, start your marketing plan (see page 81). Even if you don't feel quite ready, jump to page 81 and take the incredibly easy first baby steps you'll find there.

TIP: Since selling books will have an impact on your income tax, don't forget to talk to a small business accountant about how to prepare for that. Also, your region will have specific rules about sales tax that you'll want to learn.

NOTES:

NOTES:

FINDING THE PERFECT BOOK TITLE

(NONFICTION) IN 3 STEPS

Don't fret if you're struggling to find the perfect title for your book. After all, it's an extremely important decision: if your book title fails to be interesting, who will want to read it?

STEP 1: WHY DO YOU NEED A BOOK TITLE?

First, understand that the book title's big job is to connect your book to its readers.

That's marketing. Your book title is a marketing decision.

If you didn't want to share your book with anyone, you wouldn't even need a title for it, right?

To connect with readers, the title needs to:

☐ Distinguish your book from other books

☐ Convey what kind of book it is and what it's about (without giving too much away)

☐ Make people curious

YOUR BOOK TITLE ALSO NEEDS TO BE:

☐ Concise (e.g., don't repeat words in the title/subtitle)

☐ Memorable

BONUS POINTS IF:

☐ It contains great keywords to make your book more "discoverable"

☐ The URL is available (that is, if you want a website for your book)

☐ It's easy to say out loud

TIP: In my experience, a strong book title (combined with professional cover design) makes promotion a bit easier simply because *people will get more excited about your book if it's compelling*. Imagine if someone asked you to review their book – if the title/cover design were really strong, would you be more inclined to say yes?

THE POWER OF THE TITLE+SUBTITLE COMBO

To accomplish all of this, we have two tools: the title and the subtitle.

THE TITLE

You can be weird, wonderful, and even slightly cryptic (intriguing) with the title – then use the subtitle to clarify things like what the book is actually about, why anyone should read it, and the point of the book.

THE SUBTITLE

Nonfiction books almost always have subtitles. The subtitle can be descriptive about how the reader can expect to benefit from reading your book and/or what they may learn.

EXAMPLE

POP!: Create the Perfect Pitch, Title, and Tagline for Anything (Sam Horn)

Now that we know what we're aiming for, let's have some fun!

STEP 2: PLAY

Now you're going to immerse yourself in the creative energy of some of the most ingenious and successful nonfiction book titles available on the planet. Let's marinate your brain in excellent nonfiction book titles.

If you start to get fatigued at any point during these activities, take a break!

ACTIVITY 1: BOOK TITLE RESEARCH

Fire up your browser and peruse nonfiction books. Write down all the titles/subtitles that jump out at you (at least 20).

ACTIVITY 2: PICK ONE WORD

EXAMPLE

Limitless: Upgrade Your Brain, Learn Anything Faster, and Unlock Your Exceptional Life (Jim Kwik)

Can you think of **ONE WORD** that summarizes the main ideas of your book? By any chance does it make an intriguing book title?

ACTIVITY 3: PICK ONE PHRASE

EXAMPLES

White Fragility: Why It's So Hard for White People to Talk About Racism (Robin DiAngelo)

Can you think of **ONE SHORT PHRASE** that summarizes your book?

Think Again: The Power of Knowing What You Don't Know (Adam Grant)

When the Body Says No: The Cost of Hidden Stress (Gabor Maté)

ACTIVITY 4: YOUR SPECIAL SYSTEM/METHOD

Do you have a special name for a method, process, or system you use with your clients? This could make a fantastic title for your book. As one of my mentors says, people want to buy books (and learn from) those who have figured out *a solution to their problem.*

EXAMPLES

One Book Millions Method: How to Grow a 7-Figure Business Using One Short Book (Mike Shreeve)

Clever Girl Finance: Ditch Debt, Save Money and Build Real Wealth (Bola Sokunbi)

ACTIVITY 5: ASK A QUESTION

Is there a compelling question you can ask that summarizes the main ideas of your book?

EXAMPLE

The Universe Speaks, Are You Listening?: 111 High-Vibrational Oracle Messages on Love, Healing, and Existence to Unlock Your Inner Light (Cassady Cayne)

ACTIVITY 6: FEELINGS

If you had to describe the way you want your readers to feel when they read your book, what words would you choose?

ACTIVITY 7: CONTRAST/SURPRISE

Is there something unexpected, surprising or oppositional you can say that would tickle the reader's brain?

EXAMPLES

*Everything is F*cked: A Book about Hope* (Mark Manson)

Health At Every Size: The Surprising Truth About Your Weight (Linda Bacon)

ACTIVITY 8: BENEFITS – THE SUBTITLE

After someone reads your book, how will their life be better?

If you could wave a magic wand, what would your readers be able to do/be/have?

What interesting benefits can you think of that your reader will get from reading your book?

Is there one really strong and significant main benefit or promise you can make to your reader?

Pretend you're writing a short letter to a stranger – how would you summarize why they should bother to read it?

EXAMPLES

The Fun of Baking Bread: Impress Your Guests, Teach Your Kids & Never Buy Bagged Bread Again
(Andrea Schmidt)

Every Moment Matters: How the World's Best Coaches Inspire Their Athletes and Build Championship Teams
(John O'Sullivan)

NOTES:

ACTIVITY 9: PUT IT ALL TOGETHER – YOUR "WORKING TITLE/SUBTITLE"

Keep track of all your best title and subtitle ideas here so you can see the progress of your ideas.

STEP 3: GET OUT OF THE WAY

Once you have two or three titles that you like, it's time to ask potential readers what they think. *You may need to repeat step #2 (see page 12) a few times until you find a title that starts to click.*

MARKET RESEARCH

Find some potential readers of your book and ask them what they think of your ideas. Seek out specific people who are likely to enjoy and benefit from your book. There may already be an entire Facebook group of people to help you! Share your top title ideas with these potential readers and prepare to be astonished by how much people absolutely love to be asked for their opinions!

BONUS POINTS: By doing this research, you're simultaneously starting to build excitement and anticipation for your book. Bravo!

NOTES:

BOOK COVER RESEARCH
YOUR HOMEWORK

People judge books by the cover. Whether or not you are planning to hire an experienced book cover designer* to help you create your book cover, the book cover design has some incredibly important jobs to do.

In a nutshell: a professionally designed, intriguing book cover won't (by itself) guarantee book sales, but a poorly designed book cover will almost certainly deter (or prevent) book sales.

I believe that the most common mistake made by self-publishing authors is to underestimate the importance of having a professional-looking book cover, thinking that it's easy to do and that they can do it themselves.

Especially *online* where everyone is scanning all the time, your cover has three important functions it must fulfill, quickly.

☐ **ORIENT THE READER:** The title and the design must work harmoniously to convey immediately what type of book it is. The cover must be "on genre."

☐ **CONVEY CREDIBILITY:** The cover must demonstrate an adequate level of professionalism and avoid signals of "amateurism" that are widespread in self-publishing. Some obvious signals of professionalism include skillful treatment and handling of type and images.

☐ **ATTRACT THE READER BY BEING INTRIGUING:** This is the most challenging design objective of all. All design has the potential to be clever, inspiring, delightful, beautiful, provocative and/or magical, signalling to the reader that this book is extra special and worth reaching for – out of more than 1.4 million self-published books every year. An excellent book cover design is worth striving for, especially if you're self publishing! When a book cover makes you pause and smile, bingo.

If the cover of your book doesn't do these three basic things, people may get confused or bored, and almost certainly not buy it.

Read more about good book design on my website: **BIT.LY/GOODBOOKDESIGN**.

YOUR HOMEWORK: THE BRIEF

Time to begin the exciting phase of research for the design of your book cover! Your answers to the questions that follow will help both you and your book cover designer understand and communicate how your book can look credible, compelling and "on-genre." In design lingo, you'll be creating what is sometimes referred to as the "design brief."

---

* Here I offer my professional services! Some of you reading this are already my clients (*I love you!*). For those of you who are not, please feel free to review my book design portfolio **A-SCHMIDT.COM/DESIGN-PORTFOLIO** and consider working with me. -*Andrea*

STEP 1: COMPARABLE TITLES RESEARCH

Open your browser and set a timer for 40 minutes. Dedicate the time to browsing covers of books that are **COMPARABLE TO YOURS**.

Grab a coffee or tea. Enjoy this time.

Try not to get too distracted by the actual books themselves.

For the book covers that catch your eye, copy and paste the links into a new document (or write down the titles here). You're going to share these with your book designer to help them understand what covers you really like.

Along the way, you'll see other nonfiction book covers you like of related subject matter; keep track of those as well.

STEP 2: MORE QUESTIONS

To get the best results possible from your book designer, share the answers to these questions with them.

QUESTION 1: BRANDING
Do you have any existing brand assets (e.g., a logo or colour palette) that could potentially be incorporated strategically into your book's cover design?

QUESTION 2: PERSONAL PREFERENCES / VISION
Do you have any specific ideas, images, colours or preferences the book designer should know before getting started? What about things you hate?

Having answers to these questions ahead of time will help make the cover design process smoother and more enjoyable! Although the opinions and preferences of your target readers are of primary importance for any book cover design, **YOU** *are the final decision maker here. So it's important that the designer know your thoughts and ideas before beginning design work.*

QUESTION 3: YOUR READERS
Please describe the people who will be attracted to your book in as much detail as possible (if you're not sure yet, please see page 63).

STEP 3: COVER DESIGN TIME!

Now it's time to either hire a book cover designer or begin designing the book cover yourself.

If you are hiring or have already hired someone, compile all your homework from this section and email it to them.

To learn book cover design, there are many excellent classes and tutorials available online. You may want to design your own book cover if you are experienced in and understand (or want to learn):

- Principles of design
- Typography (skills that make text look good)
- A variety of software (e.g., Adobe InDesign, Photoshop, Illustrator, Canva)
- Image resolution requirements for different media (e.g., print and screen)
- The difference between the two main types of graphics (vector and raster)
- Colour mode requirements for different platforms (e.g., CMYK for print and RGB for screen)

Otherwise, review my portfolio and work with me or another experienced book cover designer. I started designing nonfiction publications for the University of British Columbia in 2003 and since then I have only come to love it more.

QUALITIES TO LOOK FOR IN A BOOK COVER DESIGNER:

- **YOU LIKE THEIR WORK!** Every designer has different strengths. You must review their portfolio and see whether the level of quality you are hoping for is realistic based on their body of work.
- They have experience designing book covers (this sounds obvious but many graphic designers haven't done this before and it is a unique skill set, especially if the client is self-publishing).
- **BONUS POINTS** if they can help you with your book's interior (designing and formatting the inside of your book); this simplifies the book production process for you. Once that's done, they can easily create an Advance Review Copy for you, on request (see page 43). It's also a huge bonus if they can answer your many questions about self-publishing.

WHERE TO FIND A BOOK COVER DESIGNER:

- Join and ask about this in Facebook groups for self-publishing authors
- Ask your book coach and editor
- Search on LinkedIn
- And yes, here again I do offer my help. Please review my book design portfolio **A-SCHMIDT.COM/DESIGN-PORTFOLIO** and reach out.

RECEIVING BOOK COVER MOCKUPS
NOW THE REAL FUN BEGINS!

Receiving your book cover mockups is usually an exciting part of the process: things are starting to get real!

This section assumes you are working with a professional book designer.

What is a design mockup? Also sometimes called a "comp," a mockup is a design prototype for you to review. Usually you'll receive around two to three cover designs (depending on your agreement with the designer).

Here are some tips for what to do when you receive your book cover design mockups.

- Take note of your first impressions, since these are extremely important for book sales.
- Ask yourself which cover "resonates" most and why.
- Ask trusted people in your life for their thoughts (taking everyone's opinions with a grain of salt).
- In particular, ask as many people as you can who actually belong to your target audience: these are the opinions that matter most.
- Share your favourite covers with your Book Launch Support Team (see next section). That really starts to get people excited for you and your book.
- Remember when you're reviewing your mockups on a screen that every screen displays colour differently. The printed colours may look entirely different from how they display on a screen.

For my clients, I create a "Which Cover Do You Like Best?" graphic to make it easy for them to request cover design input on social media.

BUILDING ANTICIPATION

Importantly, asking people for their opinions about your book cover design starts to generate excitement for your book. Think of excitement as the fuel for your book launch.

It's helpful to seize this moment (sometimes referred to as the "cover reveal") as a key opportunity for your book's pre-launch campaign (see page 43)!

MORE ANTICIPATION!

The topic of building excitement and anticipation leads directly to the next section – creating a book launch support team.

DESIGN REVISIONS AND FINALIZING THE COVER

At this point in the process, you'll have the opportunity to a) carefully review the input you received, mull everything over and b) request some revisions from the designer (e.g., two to three rounds is probably average) to one of the cover designs.

For example, if you love the way the type looks on one design, you can ask the designer if they can use that design element on a different mockup. In this way, the cover evolves and develops. This usually takes a week or two.

NOTES:

CREATE A BOOK LAUNCH SUPPORT TEAM (BLAST)

This is a group you (optionally) set up to help support you through the pre-launch and launch campaign of your book. I call it a BLAST but that's just my own terminology. You may hear people referring to a "street team" which is similar.

Everyone's group will be unique, depending on how and why you choose to use it. Your group can help you remember how supported you really are as you venture out of your comfort zone.

Getting this group set up is a fun way to start creating real world excitement and desire for your upcoming book in a safe environment. Creating a book launch support team for yourself is a powerful way of committing to the Universe that this is really happening.

WHEN TO CREATE YOUR BLAST

You can do this anytime, but there are (at least) a few significant decisions your group may be able to help you with: choosing the perfect title for your book, or choosing your book cover design mockups (page 23). Asking for your group's input on either of these decisions can be a fun way to introduce everyone to your book and get them pumped!

STEP 1: WHO ARE THE "VIPS" IN YOUR LIFE?

Brainstorm everyone you can think of who actively supports you in your life, including Mom, Dad, siblings, your spouse, special relatives, BFFs, book-related service providers (e.g., your editor, book designer, life coach, business mentors, etc.).

What about angels, ancestors, or guides? God? The Universe? Yes! Put everyone and everything you can think of on your list that feels supportive. Even pets if you feel like it. You are loved and supported!

Return to (and add to) this list regularly as you remember more people who are invested in you and your work.

MY VIPS ❤

NOTES:

CREATE A BOOK LAUNCH SUPPORT TEAM (BLAST), CONT.

STEP 2: WHAT KIND OF SUPPORT WILL YOU NEED?

Don't worry now if you're not exactly sure what you need from your team. This will become clear as you move forward, and it will be different for everyone.

By inviting people to join your group, you're providing a unique opportunity for people to be part of your achievement. Trust that if they say yes, they want to be there with you!

These requests may include (but are not limited to):

- Supporting you when you're freaking out
- Helping you choose a book title, cover design, etc.
- Sharing and liking your social media posts
- Answering occasional spelling or grammar questions (some people LOVE to be asked about these things!)
- Purchasing the ebook for $.99 during launch week and giving it a quick review

ANY MORE IDEAS?

STEP 3: SETTING UP THE GROUP

Depending on your preferences and comfort level with technology and social media, you have a few options about how to communicate with your BLAST. I recommend creating a private Facebook group called something like "[Your Name]'s Book Launch Support Team." Facebook groups are free, accessible, and linked to your business/author page. In order to set up the group, you would first need a Facebook author (or business) page, which is a good idea in any case.

Keep it as simple as you like. Apart from a Facebook group, you could alternatively try:

- A WhatsApp group thread
- Google Hangouts
- A simple email chain (making sure to hide people's individual emails by using the "BCC" field for privacy)

STEP 4: THE INVITE

Now we make a simple request to each person we want to invite. For example:

> *"Hi [Friend]! How are you? Guess what? I'm writing a book! The working title is [title here]. The estimated launch date is [rough date of launch here]. Are you willing to support me in my journey of launching it? For example: moral support, sharing my announcements? If you are willing to be a part of my book launch support team, it would mean a lot to me. And if you'd rather not, no worries at all!"*

NOTES:

CREATE A BOOK LAUNCH SUPPORT TEAM (BLAST), CONT.

If asking for help is a challenge for you (as it is for me), use the process of launching your book as an opportunity to practice this valuable life skill.

TIPS:

This is personal: Ask people individually.

Specificity: When asking for help, I've found it is extremely helpful to be as specific as possible about what you're asking for, thereby making it as easy as possible for people to understand what they're saying yes or no to.

Outcome independence: In all ways, it's best to ask without expectation. We ask, and (of course) people are free to say yes or no.

Appreciation: Make sure to include all members of your BLAST in your book's Acknowledgments. Keep an eye out for other ways to show appreciating for them, e.g., thank you card, shout out on social media, signed copy of your book. They are VIPs after all.

NOTES:

INTERIOR BOOK DESIGN AND FORMATTING

There comes a time when every self-publishing author must figure out how to transform their manuscript (which is probably written in a word processing software like MS Word) into the file formats required for self-publishing to various platforms (ebook and/or paperback).

Even if you're not completely done writing your book, it might be worthwhile to think ahead to these important decisions now.

This is an area where people get easily confused and frustrated, so it's important to know a few basics:

- The tools and skills required to create a book layout file for print (e.g., paperback) are generally different than those required to create an ebook. They are very different beasts.
- Print-on-Demand (POD) is an impressive innovation that allows us to order and print small batches of books (e.g., one book, in some cases), as opposed to a minimum quantity print order of thousands. POD is the basis for all self-publishing platforms offering printed books. The quality of these POD books is usually decent and acceptable, but lower than books printed via offset lithography. POD books are produced very quickly. To give you an idea, *this* nice book you're holding in your hands is printed through POD.
- If your book has a colour interior (e.g., a children's picture book, a coffee table book, or a cookbook), it will be somewhat expensive per book to produce. Self-publishing platforms are optimal for books with a black ink interior.
- If your book has charts, tables, a lot of graphics, and/or an index, it will also be more challenging and time-consuming to prepare for self-publishing (either as a paperback or an ebook) and will require a custom interior.

Unless you already have a background in desktop publishing and/or website design or you really want to learn some new skills, there are no simple straightforward solutions to all your questions.

However, if you feel up to the challenge of formatting your own books (in particular if they are extremely simple, text-only books), formatting your own books will save you money and allow you to update the content of your books whenever you want for free.

OPTIONS

- Hire professionals
- Learn some new skills and invest in software (desktop publishing and/or ebook creation)
- On Amazon KDP, try the Kindle Create tool
- Try the formatting tools on D2D or Reedsy
- Wrangle with MS Word
- **TIP**: Join some self-publishing Facebook groups in order to have lots of kind, smart people answer your questions – for free – within minutes

There is a learning curve for all software, so consider both the time it would take you to learn these skills and the cost of the software itself. If you go this route, there are many excellent courses available online.

NOTES:

INTERIOR BOOK DESIGN AND FORMATTING, CONT.

SOFTWARE I USE

As a graphic designer for over 20 years, I have a monthly subscription to Adobe Creative Cloud in order to access the industry-standard software required to create custom covers and interiors of books. Primarily, I use Adobe InDesign, Photoshop, and Illustrator. For creating simple ebooks, I (currently) use a software called Vellum.

INTERIOR BOOK DESIGN

Whenever you're ready with a sample chapter from your manuscript (it doesn't have to be a final draft), email it to your designer so they can create some interior mockups (book styles) for you to review and choose from.

REVIEW TIPS:

After you receive interior book samples, make a list of any questions you may have.

Working with me on a simple book interior (mostly text, no index, minimal graphics and charts), only minor customizations are possible to the interior. The reason for that is that (often) I'm using a software called Vellum, which creates interior book files for both ebooks and paperback (streamlining the process). Some design style options for the book interior include choices of fonts, justification, running headers, and how the chapter heading pages are styled.

EBOOK REVIEW

Make sure to thoroughly review your ebook files before they are published. If you prefer to do this on your desktop, download the Kindle Previewer (free). Search "Kindle Previewer [Mac or Windows]" and install the software.

QUESTIONS AND NOTES:

NOTES:

INTERIOR BOOK DESIGN AND FORMATTING, CONT.

TIP: As you know if you're an ebook reader, users of ebooks can tailor their book style settings on their specific devices. For this reason, design elements you see when reviewing your ebook (e.g., font) will be *default settings* only.

WHEN YOUR MANUSCRIPT IS READY

Hurray! Your manuscript is complete and you can send it to your formatter or format it yourself.

In order to minimize excess changes once interior layout begins, please make sure the manuscript is thoroughly copyedited and proofread before your formatter receives it.

FIRST DRAFT REVIEW

Once the interior is formatted, you'll receive the first full draft of your interior – possibly for both ebook and paperback.

You'll need to carefully review both.

COMMUNICATING REVISIONS

As you read through the first draft, keep a list of changes you'd like to see made. Depending on your agreement, you may get two to three rounds of revisions to the layout after this point.

QUESTIONS AND NOTES:

NOTES:

SOME EYE-WATERINGLY BORING STUFF YUP

This is a checklist of nerdy book decisions. Largely administrative, you may want to consider getting an assistant to help you out here. *Under no circumstances should you get bogged down with these details!*

ORDERING ISBNs

For an author who is taking their book seriously, it's good practice to acquire your own International Standard Book Number (ISBN). This allows you to be identified as the publisher of your book. For example, if you decide to use one of the free ISBNs provided by one of the self-publishing platforms for your paperback, you may save a few bucks (in the case of US self-publishers), but Amazon will be listed as the "publisher," and you won't be able to sell that paperback anywhere but on Amazon (because the ISBN will be *tied to Amazon*).

One ISBN is required for each format of your book (e.g., paperback, ebook, audiobook, hard cover). The process for acquiring ISBNs is specific to what country you live in.

ISBNS IN THE UNITED STATES
☐ For US self-publishers, order your ISBNs from Bowker, where they come in packs of 1 or 10.

Tip from Bowker:

> "Inputting the title: The 'title' field is the identifying name given to a published work. Enter the full title in mixed case exactly as it appears on the title page of the book. Do not include additional information such as subtitle, order number, edition number, volume number, etc., in the title. Example: For 'The History of Madison County: 200 Years of Agriculture,' the title is 'The History of Madison County' and the subtitle is '200 Years of Agriculture.'"

RECAP: Make sure to put your title and subtitle in separate fields when you assign your ISBN in Bowker (as above). Then, be very consistent about how you fill in these fields everywhere else (e.g., on KDP, Goodreads etc).

ISBNS IN CANADA
☐ Canadians get their ISBNs for free from Library and Archives Canada:
WWW.BAC-LAC.GC.CA/ENG/SERVICES/ISBN-CANADA

It may take a week or two until your account is set up. After that, you'll easily be able to create and edit ISBNs.

DO I NEED TO BUY A BARCODE?

☐ No – there's no need to purchase a barcode for the back cover of your paperback. Your cover designer can create that for you as soon as you tell them your ISBN number.

PUBLISHER NAME (AKA IMPRINT)

☐ What is your "publisher" name? Who will be "the publisher"? You can use your name. Or you can set up a publishing "Imprint" (talk to your accountant about the tax implications). Please keep track of what name you choose. *This becomes important later for consistency when it's time to upload your paperback files (e.g., Amazon cross-checks the ISBN from Bowker and everything must match exactly).*

BOOK PRICES

☐ You'll need to choose prices for your book(s).

If you research this topic, you'll find a lot of information and formulas. However, you can keep it simple by researching books comparable to yours, and pricing similarly (or slightly higher). Slightly higher pricing for printed books allows you to (potentially) offer a discount to bookstores (see page 87),

NOTES:

SOME EYE-WATERINGLY BORING STUFF, CONT.

create higher "perceived value," and offset shipping costs. But of course you'll need to balance that with what people will actually pay for the book.

☐ You'll also need to decide whether you want the price embedded in your barcode and included on the back cover of the printed book.

SHORT ANSWER: Many self-publishers choose not to put a price on the book. However, if you think you might want to sell your book through a bookstore (see page 87) at some point (or at least keep the option open), some bookstores require a price embedded in the barcode, so there's no downside to including it. Plus it looks extra professional to include it. Read more here: **HTTP://BIT.LY/EMBEDPRICE**

REQUEST A PRE-ASSIGNED CONTROL NUMBER

☐ For US self-publishers only, this is optional. Pre-Assigned Control Numbers are a unique identification number you can choose to request for your book in order to help librarians who end up with your book in their hands. Although I am honestly not sure whether it's worth the effort to do this, I suspect most people do it because it's both free and straightforward. Information available here: **HTTPS://WWW.LOC.GOV/PUBLISH/PCN**.

PRIMARY BISAC CATEGORY

☐ Choose a BISAC category for the back cover.

If you study the back of nonfiction books, you'll often see a word or phrase included that indicates the book's major category (e.g., WOMEN'S HEALTH). Ask yourself: where in the bookstore would you want your book to go, based on the categories you'll find here: **HTTPS://BISG.ORG/PAGE/BISACEDITION**.

RESEARCH SELF-PUBLISHING PLATFORMS

☐ Where will you upload and sell your book? Because Amazon dominates the book-selling market, most people take advantage of Amazon's KDP self-publishing platform, and sometimes Ingram-Spark as well (see page 87). If you're already familiar with these platforms and want to expand your book's reach, you can choose to "go wide" with your distribution (see page 87).

RESEARCH YOUR OWN ONLINE SALES SYSTEM

☐ With some planning, consider selling your book through your own online system, e.g., on your website or through what's called a book sales funnel.

A book funnel is designed to generate leads for your business, offering "upsells" to your other services and products (see page 83).

In either of these cases, you'll need to: a) either hire a web developer or funnel building team (including a sales copywriter), or b) attempt it yourself, and c) find a way to drive traffic to your page, usually done through online advertising. This is a lot of hard work, especially for a new author.

SET UP YOUR KDP AND/OR INGRAMSPARK ACCOUNT(S)

☐ If you plan to offer your book for sale through Amazon's KDP, IngramSpark etc., you'll need to set up those accounts with your banking information so you can receive your royalties.

I always insist that my clients set up their own accounts so they can receive their royalties directly and have access to their own book listings. There are service providers out there who will happily "do it all for you" – *however, this is one step that I highly recommend you always do for yourself.*

NOTES:

FRONT AND BACK BOOK MATTER

The terms "front and back matter" refer to small chunks of a book at the front and back. Some of these are optional, but some of them can be used strategically, e.g., to add credibility to your book.

☐ **TITLE PAGE:** Contains the full title of the book plus the name of the author. Placement is always on the right-hand side ("recto") of the book. It also has the subtitle and many times, the publisher name and city.

☐ **COPYRIGHT PAGE:** Study other comparable books and put together one for yours. Optionally, include contact information, and feel free to show some personality here. Placement is always on the left ("verso") of the book.

☐ **DEDICATION:** This book has the dedication on the bottom of the copyright page.

☐ **TABLE OF CONTENTS:** The TOC helps the reader navigate to major sections/chapters in the book. Often, the book designer's software will create a Contents page automatically for you, so you may not necessarily need to worry about generating this yourself.

☐ **PREFACE:** A statement written by the author about why they wrote the book/how it came to be/the purpose of the book. Use it show off your credentials and maybe tell a story to spark curiosity about the origins of the book.

☐ **FOREWORD:** Always written by another person, e.g., a relevant and credible expert on your book's topic – basically, a giant book endorsement. *Consider whether you know anyone who can write your foreword.*

☐ **INTRODUCTION:** Introduces the content and topics in the book and helps orient the readers as to what they can expect in the book and what they will get from reading it.

☐ **ACKNOWLEDGMENTS:** Nowadays, this section is often placed at the back of the book. Traditionally it was placed in the front. Take your time with this, and include as many people as you can. Make a plan to contact each person individually to let them know the positive impact they've had on your work. In many cases, they will be delighted that you've written a book, and that they've been acknowledged!

☐ **EPILOGUE:** A brief conclusion of the book's content.

☐ **ABOUT THE AUTHOR:** The author bio can go at the back of the book and/or (a shorter version) on the back cover of the paperback.

☐ **A FEW OTHER BACK MATTER SECTIONS:** Endnotes, bibliography, glossary, index which may or may not be necessary. These items go in a specific order according to Chicago Manual of Style.

TIPS:

- To help you decide how (and whether you want to) create each section, study other books comparable to yours and see how other publishers handle them.

- Make sure all these sections get edited and proofread carefully before being sent for formatting.

NOTES:

ADVANCE REVIEWS: SOCIAL PROOF

WHAT IS AN ARC AND WHAT IS IT FOR?

I always try my best to get advance review blurbs for my books, and I highly recommend you try as well.

Once you have a nice clean draft of your book formatted (and the book cover finalized), you can make a significant effort to get advance reviews (also known as "social proof") for your book by sending out Advance Review Copies (also known as ARCs).

For a number of reasons, many self-publishers skip this step entirely.

Firstly, it's challenging to get people to respond. Don't underestimate the amount of attention and care that must be taken in order to persuade a busy person to do you the favour of reading (or skimming) and reviewing your book. Please don't get discouraged if your efforts seem futile.

Secondly, some people believe that it's only worthwhile to get blurbs from famous people. I disagree with this perspective – I believe that if someone you respect is willing to take the time to write a review blurb for your book, then that is wonderful and helpful. Of course, do try to get the most credible people possible to review your book!

SOCIAL PROOF

Think about the last thing you bought online. Unless you were searching directly for a specific item you were sure you already wanted to buy, you probably scanned the reviews before buying it.

Most people rely on social proof in order to buy anything online.

For books, review "blurbs" (as they're sometimes called) are found in quite a few different places: the back cover of a paperback or hardcover, sometimes on the front cover, on the website sales page, in at least two different places on the Amazon sales page, and sometimes even at the very beginning of a book, in a "Praise" section.

Having review blurbs is a subtle and powerful way to prove that your book is worth reading and buying. Cues like this add up to help motivate people to reach for your book.

WHAT IS AN ADVANCE REVIEW COPY (ARC)?

Getting reviews BEFORE the book is published may seem backward. How do we do it?

An Advance Review Copy (ARC) or Advance Reader's Copy (ARC) is a copy of your book you send out to readers in advance of publishing, with a request that they read and review it.

Practically speaking for indie authors, this will usually be a PDF of your book that you attach to an email. I suppose you could also send out a Word document, especially if you're sending it to someone you know well. Another option: mail out a printed copy (see page 77 to find out more).

If you're working with an experienced book designer, let them know that you want an ARC, and they can create this for you (including a watermark on the PDF indicating that the book is an ARC).

NOTES:

ADVANCE REVIEWS: SOCIAL PROOF, CONT.

HOW TO GET ADVANCE REVIEWS: ASKING PEOPLE YOU KNOW

STEP 1: BRAINSTORM PEOPLE YOU KNOW

Brainstorm friends, colleagues, friends of friends, old friends you know (or can figure out how to contact) who may be interested in your book, or who are supportive and like to help. People with whom you have goodwill.

These people can be in your industry – but they don't need to be. They can be in a related industry, or perhaps they are an author (of a related book), or simply have an interest.

Take your time and keep adding to your list as you think of people. Remember your retired aunt who is interested in the subject matter of your book? Or your best friend's dad who (you just remembered) cares about the subject matter of your book? Gather up a list of people who may legitimately care about what you are doing. Kind people who will benefit from and enjoy your book.

Consider the teachers and mentors who have had a positive impact on your life. Are there any you could reach out to and thank? Potentially include in your Acknowledgments section?

If so, let them know! They will be delighted to hear from you, and perhaps willing to write an advance review. It doesn't hurt to ask.

TIP: Make a note of anyone you'd like to send a print copy of your book to.

STEP 2: FIRST ASK – PLANTING A SEED

Contact each person on your list individually and invite them to write a short blurb for the back cover of your book. If you don't have their email, try to connect with them through LinkedIn, Facebook, Twitter, etc.

PEOPLE TO ASK ❤

NOTES:

ADVANCE REVIEWS: SOCIAL PROOF, CONT.

TIP: I find that people are generally not interested in (or don't have time) to write a review for a book. So if you find someone willing to do it, make sure to thank them properly! I find emailing people directly to be the most effective way to communicate with people about advance reviews. However, there are other ways people do it: create a landing page, or try a more automated online service such as Book-Funnel: HTTPS://AUTHORS.BOOKFUNNEL.COM *(which I haven't tried)*.

Here's the first email template (feel free to copy and/or adapt this):

> Dear [Friend],
>
> How are you doing? I know it's been awhile! I hope you are well, and [something personal here]!
>
> Would you please consider writing me a short, honest blurb for the back cover of my upcoming [genre here] book?
>
> The title of my upcoming book is:
>
> [Title here]
>
> If you are willing, I could potentially email an advance copy to you by [date]. A few sentences would be totally fine!
>
> Thank you so much for considering it!
>
> *Here's an example: "This is a delightful book full of powerful ideas, which helped me... Reading it will definitely improve your..." – Your Name/Title/Your Business*
>
> Sincerely, [You]

STEP 3: SECOND ASK

Send the Advance Review Copy ARC – make sure to attach the PDF of your book.

Here's a template for the second "ask":

> Hi!
>
> Thank you so much for your interest and support! I am thrilled that you wouldn't mind taking a peek at my book.
>
> An "Advance Review Copy" of [Book Title here] is attached.
>
> *Again, here's another example: "After I read this book, I saw things differently. I like how this book helped me ... When I read it, I really..." – Your Name / Title / Your Business*
>
> It would be incredibly helpful if you could write a few sentences for the back cover of my book by [date here].
>
> Thank you again so much!
>
> Sincerely, [You]

NOTES:

ADVANCE REVIEWS: SOCIAL PROOF, CONT.

STEP 4: FOLLOW-UP

Here's a third follow-up email template:

> Hello,
>
> Hope this finds you well! Thank you so much for supporting my book [title of book here].
>
> It's launching on [date] – do you have a sentence or two for me to include? I am happy to proofread whatever you write.
>
> Thank you again so much!
>
> Sincerely, [You]

ASKING PEOPLE YOU DON'T KNOW

Create a list of "dream reviewers" – influential people in your industry. Asking people you don't know for an advance review (e.g., people in your field who are well-known and highly credible as experts) is similar to the previous method, but takes more patience and ingenuity. This is because you'll have to figure out a way to contact them, and you'll need to be extra persuasive (since you're a stranger to them).

LINKEDIN

Assuming you've already tried and failed at Googling their contact info, the best way to reach people is often through LinkedIn.

Even if you can't find contact information for the person you're looking for, you might find contact info for someone on their publicity or communications team by searching their name.

FACEBOOK

Facebook is another great channel that *sometimes* allows you to communicate with people you don't know.

If you join some Facebook groups based on the subject of your book, you will inevitably meet people interested in your book.

TIP: Go into groups with a helping mindset. Be patient, friendly, helpful, and persistent. You never know what new friends you could make.

PEOPLE TO ASK ♥

NOTES:

PROMOTIONAL COPY

You thought you were done writing… Almost! One of the benefits of choosing the self-publishing path is that you can promote your business goals more overtly throughout your book (than if you were being traditionally published).

Take advantage of that opportunity by writing and including some self-promotional text throughout the book.

These first two sections are expected, but the rest are optional.

ABOUT THE AUTHOR – YOUR BIO

☐ **YOUR AUTHOR BIO:** Although this was already mentioned (see page 41), consider creating both a short bio (for the back cover), and a longer version for the back of the book. You'll need this text later for your website, press release, Amazon Author page, etc. as well.

BACK COVER DESCRIPTION

☐ **BACK COVER DESCRIPTION FOR PRINT EDITION(S):** The back cover description (or "blurb" as it's sometimes called) needs to connect the potential buyer with all the reasons they should buy your book (the benefits). For this copywriting task, you may be able to go back to some of the hard work you did on page 15. See if you can incorporate some of the benefits you came up with then, or come up with new ones, turning them into bullet points. For inspiration, use the Internet to research back cover descriptions of other comparable top-selling books. Read books on the subject, e.g., *How to Write a Sizzling Synopsis* by Bryan Cohen. Or hire a copywriter. The back cover description is usually around 150 words. Use the swipe file to keep track of your ideas (see page 104).

TIP: Many authors use this copy for the book description sections required on self-publishing platforms.

ENTICING READERS TO JOIN YOUR EMAIL LIST

☐ **"GET YOUR FREE GIFT AT [LINK HERE]…"**

Offering a bonus gift (e.g., a PDF) to your readers is a way of enticing them to join your email list so you can communicate with them after they've finished your book. If you already have an email list set up and running, congratulations. If not, setting up an email list and enticing readers to join is a significant project involving a number of moving parts.

HOW TO DO IT: The three main things that need to be in place: an email list (e.g., sign up for an account with Mailchimp or MailerLite etc.) and a landing page (a special type of web page) that allows visitors to download a file (sometimes called a "lead magnet") once they provide their email address. Another alternative is to use a digital marketing platform: e.g., ClickFunnels or DropFunnels. This may require some advance planning with your website designer and/or (potentially) a copywriter and email marketing professional.

Building an email list allows you to stay in touch with your readers after they've bought your book (thereby creating potentially new business relationships and adding to your credibility).

PRAISE

☐ **"PRAISE FOR [BOOK NAME HERE]"**

If you get Advance Reviews (see page 43), ask your book designer to include a "Praise" section at the very beginning (before the title page).

NOTES:

PROMOTIONAL COPY CONT.

CONNECT WITH THE AUTHOR SECTION

☐ **"CONNECT WITH THE AUTHOR [SOCIAL MEDIA LINKS/ WEBSITE HERE]."** People love to connect directly with the author of a powerful book they just read!

HOW TO DO IT: At the end of your book (and on the back cover of your book), include links to your author social media accounts and website. To be as considerate as possible to your readers (especially if you're including this in or on your paperback books), use "short links," e.g., bit.ly (or others) when necessary.

REQUEST FOR REVIEWS

☐ **"IF YOU ENJOYED THIS BOOK, PLEASE LEAVE A QUICK, HONEST REVIEW AT THE WEBSITE WHERE YOU PURCHASED THE BOOK."**

Because reviews are so important for sales, make it as easy as possible for people who love your book to remember to give it a quick, honest review.

HOW TO DO IT: I often include this text on both the copyright page of the paperback and at the end of the book. If you can, include shortened links to your book sales page, as well as clear instructions to help the reader, e.g., "Click on this link and then scroll down to the *Write a Customer Review* button."

Many people will just ignore the request. However, a few may appreciate the reminder and leave you a nice review.

OTHER BOOKS BY YOU, THE AUTHOR

☐ **"OTHER BOOKS BY..."** If you've written other books, include a page that tells your reader what they are and where they can find them.

NOTES:

NOTES:

THE BACK COVER AND SPINE
OF YOUR PRINTED BOOK

For most printed books, the cover file is one long (horizontal) print-ready PDF which gets printed and trimmed before the book is bound.

The back cover of a printed book contains some important elements. Here is a checklist of items (some are required and some are optional) for the back cover of your book. Many of these have already been mentioned.

☐ **ISBN** – Assuming you've purchased your own ISBN, now your designer will transform it into a barcode (using an online barcode generator) and plop it on the back cover.

☐ **BOOK PRICE** – If you've decided to include your book's price on the back cover, the designer will need to know that information now (in all the currencies you'd like to include – e.g., for US and Canadian markets, the price will typically appear for both USD and CAD). See page 37 for more info.

☐ **BACK COVER DESCRIPTION** – This section of the book focuses on how the book benefits the reader. See page 51 for more info.

☐ **PRIMARY BISAC CATEGORY** – See page 39 for more details on this. Find your category options here: HTTPS://BISG.ORG/PAGE/BISACEDITION.

☐ **SHORT AUTHOR BIO AND HEADSHOT** – It's wonderful to see the author's face on the back cover next to a short bio. A short author bio on the back cover can be around 100 words.

☐ **YOUR WEBSITE URL**

☐ **SOCIAL MEDIA HANDLES**

☐ **ADVANCE BLURBS** – If you have some strong advance blurbs, include these on the back cover.

THE BOOK SPINE

Generally, if your book is roughly 100 pages or more, the spine can have type on it. Usually a book spine has the title, author name and sometimes the publisher's name or logo.

SPINE WIDTH

How wide will the book spine be? This depends on both your book's page count, and the thickness of the book's paper stock.

If you are using either IngramSpark or KDP, the cover designer can prepare your cover file for print once you have verified the following things:

a) Which POD platform(s) you're using

b) Your book's page count

c) The book's paper stock (different paper stocks have different thicknesses).

TIP: on these platforms, the available paper stock varies depending on the dimension of your book.

In the case of KDP, you'll often get the choice between white paper (which is more common for nonfiction) or cream paper (more common for fiction). I personally like the cream paper for both fiction and nonfiction books. It's slightly thicker than the white paper.

If you are are working with a different book printing vendor than these, you'll simply ask the vendor to supply you with the spine width for your book (based on their paper stock and your page count).

NOTES:

THINKING AHEAD TO YOUR BOOK LAUNCH

WHAT IS A BOOK LAUNCH, ANYWAY?

OVERVIEW

Most authors I know (including myself) are introverted people who generally avoid attracting attention to themselves. Even the extroverted authors I know have to get used to the vulnerability required for publishing a book.

If you are writing a book and planning to offer it for sale, at some specific point in time the book will "launch" into the marketplace.

Unless you are an incredibly confident person (or a marketing professional), you may have mixed feelings about this idea of a "book launch."

What is a book launch, anyway?

- An opportunity to introduce your book to people who will enjoy and benefit from it and buy it.
- An opportunity to celebrate a magnificent achievement in your life (the completion and release of your book)!
- A time to get out of your own way and revel in the impact your book is going to have in the real world.

For a self-publishing author, a book launch is simply whatever you make it: as much or as little, on a spectrum of minimum to maximum effort.

EFFORT=BOOK SALES

Book sales are a byproduct of your efforts before (during the "pre-launch" campaign), during, and after the launch.

For self-publishers, it's up to you to decide how much of a "push" you want to give your book into the world, and how you want to do it.

Traditionally during a book launch (online or in-person), there's some kind of an event or party. Often an author reads from their new book, answers questions, signs books, sells books, gives away books, etc.

If you decide to hold a book launch event, you'll need to a) find someone to help you (see page 107), or b) plan it yourself.

Importantly, there's no one way to do this! There's lots of room for creativity and fun.

PRE-LAUNCH CAMPAIGN

In the lead-up to the book launch, efforts revolve around the goal of getting people curious and excited about your upcoming book so that the people who will benefit from and enjoy it can have the opportunity to find and buy it (see page 63).

MORE THAN JUST A "ONE-TIME" EVENT

Importantly, you'll get the most from your book launch if you think of all your efforts as part of the larger, ongoing effort of supporting your book marketing goals.

NOTES:

THINKING AHEAD TO YOUR BOOK LAUNCH, CONT.

SCARY, BUT YOU CAN DO THIS

IF I CAN DO IT, YOU CAN DO IT

When I was launching my first book, I was very much not excited about the idea of a book launch event.

And yet, the small neighbourhood book launch event I organized at my local tea shop ended up being one of my favourite memories from the entire experience, and the one that I'm definitely most proud of.

LAUNCH WEEK

Think of the book launch as a week-long period during which you'll be making sure your files are uploaded and selling, promoting your book on social media, and perhaps holding an event(s). So many options! Your creativity is the limit. Dream up something unusual that your specific audience will be excited about, and go for it.

Definitely don't let the opportunity pass by. Your book will only be *new* once!

Ideally, planning for this starts (at least) a few months in advance in order to maximize the impact of your efforts. During launch week, you'll receive a burst of strong book sales, signalling to your online sales platform (e.g., Amazon) that your book is excellent and that people like it.

DON'T FORGET: You are likely moving out of your comfort zone here, which is very valuable for personal growth. You may end up with a "vulnerability hangover" as Brené Brown talks about in her teachings. I know you may not want to do this, but it might be time to say "Hey!" to the world. That actually turns out to be less scary and more exhilarating than you know now! And every time you say "Hey!" it gets a tiny bit easier.

For obvious reasons, book launch events have largely moved online. However, you get bonus points for creatively working within your limitations to organize some kind of small, outdoor, "in-person" event to celebrate your accomplishment, even if it's just a celebratory picnic with your loved ones.

HOSTING AN EVENT

To host an event (which implies multiple people), you'll need to a) pick a venue and/or platform, and b) ideally find someone to help you – a co-host or someone to help you with managing it.

Consider Instagram Live, a multi-person Zoom meeting, or perhaps a Facebook Live event (especially if your audience is already on Facebook).

Host the book launch at your neighbourhood cafe or bookstore.

All of these ideas will require research, elbow grease, and potentially (as mentioned) stepping out of your comfort zone.

In addition to a launch event, you can plan other online activities, e.g., a crowdfunding campaign, an interview with another author or an influencer in your niche, a quiz about your book topic, etc.

Don't worry about it. Trust that you will do your best! Every action you take will build momentum. This may sound hard to believe now, but it really is exciting to finally launch your book into the world.

NOTES:

THINKING AHEAD TO YOUR BOOK LAUNCH, CONT.

SCARY, BUT YOU CAN DO THIS

TIMELINE: WORK BACKWARDS FROM THE END GOAL

For a book launch event, timing is important. You need to work backwards from the end goal. If you want to give away a paperback signed copy of the book during your event, then you need to build two or three weeks into your schedule to order and receive the printed books (see page 77).

TIP: Print or handwrite little thank you notes into these printed books, with a request to please leave a review (include the link).

NOTES:

NOTES:

GENERATING EXCITEMENT: YOUR PRE-LAUNCH CAMPAIGN

WHO ARE YOUR TARGET READERS?

A strong pre-launch campaign helps you take advantage of the brief period of time when your book is fresh and new, which is highly attractive to your readers. Who are your readers? This is a key place to begin.

As mentioned, making a book available doesn't ensure book sales. Ongoing marketing efforts are almost always required for ongoing book sales.

If you already have an audience, e.g., an email list, Instagram followers, a Facebook group (etc.), congratulations! Well done. Continue to build on your current efforts, especially if you are enjoying what you're already doing.

If not, it's never too soon to start thinking about how to connect with your readers. Now we will work on identifying who will benefit from and enjoy your book, and then connect with some of those people.

The goal of a "pre-launch campaign" is to expose people to you and your book in authentic and meaningful ways. Working backwards from that goal, let's figure out who those people are!

Take your time, but don't overthink the questions that follow. Feel free to work on just the questions that appeal to you.

It's possible that you'll have a number of different audiences who are quite different from one another. That's fine. Just write everything down you can think of.

WHO WILL ENJOY, BENEFIT FROM, AND LEARN FROM YOUR BOOK?

Efforts you put into this section now will continue to have positive residual effects later. Take your time and trust that ideas will come.

TIP: Notice if this question brings up uncomfortable feelings, e.g., anxiety, frustration, uncertainty, overwhelm. If so, there is almost certainly a good reason, perhaps related to vulnerability. Does the idea of releasing your book to the world feel risky? Be compassionate with yourself. Notice what's happening. Take deep breaths and begin!

QUESTION #1: WHY DID YOU WRITE THIS BOOK? LIST OUT ALL YOUR REASONS

QUESTION #2: ARE YOU PART OF YOUR OWN AUDIENCE FOR THIS BOOK? *If "no," skip to the next question.*

IF YES: Do you (or did you ever) need a book like this one that you've written? If so, please write down all the reasons why that is (or was) the case.

QUESTION #3: WHAT DOES YOUR BOOK HAVE THE POTENTIAL TO REALLY HELP PEOPLE WITH?

EXAMPLES: Encourage someone to love themselves more, improve their relationship, sell more books.

GENERATING EXCITEMENT:
YOUR PRE-LAUNCH CAMPAIGN, CONT.
FIND YOUR READERS

QUESTION #4: WHO ARE SOME INDIVIDUALS
(ACTUAL PEOPLE YOU KNOW) WHO MIGHT
BENEFIT FROM AND ENJOY YOUR BOOK?

QUESTION #5: WHAT OBVIOUS GROUPS OF PEOPLE MAY BENEFIT FROM AND ENJOY YOUR BOOK?

EXAMPLES: Couples, coaches, entrepreneurs, authors.

QUESTION #6: ARE THERE SMALLER (MORE SPECIFIC) GROUPS WITHIN THE PREVIOUS GROUPS?

EXAMPLES: Freelancers who are struggling to find clients, women who love romance novels and who are eager for more diverse content, authors who are self-publishing for the first time.

QUESTION #7: WHO WILL **NOT** BE INTERESTED IN YOUR BOOK?

_____

_____

_____

_____

QUESTION #8: SUMMARIZE EVERYTHING YOU'VE DISCOVERED ABOUT YOUR AUDIENCE AND WHERE YOU MIGHT FIND THEM

EXAMPLES: *Nonfiction Authors* – author groups on FB, meetup groups, self-publishing groups on FB, LinkedIn.

_____

_____

_____

_____

_____

_____

_____

_____

GENERATING EXCITEMENT:
YOUR PRE-LAUNCH CAMPAIGN, CONT.

REACHING OUT

The lead-up to your book launch gives you time to experiment with creating desire for your book in a way that feels authentic. I say "experiment" because there really is no *one way* to do this. The choices you make here are as unique as you are. Suggestions below are just the tip of the iceberg for ways you can generate excitement for your book.

TIP: Don't try to do *everything*. If you try to do everything, you may get understandably overwhelmed!

EMAIL + SPREADSHEET

Consider emailing people you know (individually) to let them know about your upcoming book. Include a screenshot or 3D graphic of the cover. Say something like:

> *"Hi [Name]! How are you doing? Guess what?! I'm writing a book about _____. It's called _____. It is launching on [Date]. Would you be interested in being in the loop about it? Is there anyone else you can think of who might benefit from my book? Thank you!"*

Keep a spreadsheet of everyone who says yes (including their contact info or social media handle). These are important people who have raised their hands to indicate that they would be interested to hear more.

Consider and plan for how you'll follow up with them: Email them again? A tag on social media? Invite them to like your Facebook Author page?

CUSTOM EMAIL VACATION NOTIFICATION

I got this idea from Nick Loper, Udemy instructor of *Kindle Launch Plan*. Turn on your email vacation notification with a note about your upcoming book. With zero effort on your part, everyone who emails you will receive this notification. *Don't forget to change the message after your book launch!*

YOUR EMAIL SIGNATURE

Put some concise (and intriguing) information about your upcoming book directly under your name in your email signature, so anyone you interact with by email has the opportunity to learn about your upcoming book.

SOCIAL MEDIA

If you're experienced with social media, you already know that the more care and attention you put in, the more likely it is that others will care back. Social media engagement is based on reciprocity and shared interests.

Audience building is a long-term endeavour. Even if you end up eventually deciding to pay for traffic through advertising, you may want to do some of this "organic" social media legwork yourself.

Whether your current audience is zero or in the thousands, it's never too early to start planning out interactions with your potential readers. Don't put too much pressure on yourself with this, or try too hard – it won't help your relationship-building efforts. Stay loose! Stay happy. Have fun with it.

TIP: After your book is launched, you'll continue to have plenty of opportunities to build friendships and connections with your readers. In many cases, your book launch is just the beginning of a new stage in your career.

If you are attempting to build an audience from scratch, just know that it may seem very slow at first… some days/months you feel as though it's

NOTES:

GENERATING EXCITEMENT: YOUR PRE-LAUNCH CAMPAIGN, CONT.

SOCIAL MEDIA

just not working. However, as long as your efforts are focused on truly helping people, there's an exponential growth curve that always starts with just a handful of people. With care and patience, your efforts will eventually be rewarded. The sooner you can jump in and start making connections with people who can potentially benefit from and enjoy your book, the better. Try to think of it as an exciting opportunity to connect with your potential readers.

Start with an inventory: what social media platforms (if any) are you already using that you like? Are there any that you at least have an account already set up for? Are there any that you are interested in trying out? Where are your friends (and importantly, where is your audience)?

Here are just a few examples of some of the platforms (which are growing daily!) on which you can engage with people:

- Twitter
- Instagram
- Your personal Facebook account (just be careful not to overuse your personal Facebook account for business activities)
- Business or author Facebook page (recommended)
- Your own Facebook group (requires a business or author page, above)
- Other people's Facebook groups
- LinkedIn
- YouTube channel
- Pinterest
- TikTok (#BookTok)
- Clubhouse

Pick out one or two platforms that you enjoy (or imagine you might enjoy) and get started! Schedule it into your day. You never know where your efforts will end up over time.

TIP: Each platform has its strengths, which is good information to know. But keep in mind that if you choose a platform solely based on its perceived strengths and then don't use it, those strengths are not going to benefit you.

To be successful – and by successful, I mean having people who are interested in you and your book, and who want to buy it – your posts must be oriented toward your reader and what they want and care about.

SOCIAL MEDIA: STRATEGY

In order to use social media as an effective tool (as opposed to being at the mercy of its wildly addictive forces), it's important to stay focused on what you're trying to accomplish and why you're even doing all this in the first place.

We want to use it to build relationships and share our book with as many people as possible.

TIPS:

a) **POST WITH AS MUCH JOY AND AUTHENTICITY AS POSSIBLE.** Post when you feel good... If you are posting out of a sense of obligation, that energy can carry through. Make sure the content you post is meaningful to both you and your audience in some way. An occasional rant can be great too, as long as you're taking a stand for something that your audience will find compelling.

NOTES:

GENERATING EXCITEMENT:
YOUR PRE-LAUNCH CAMPAIGN, CONT.

SOCIAL MEDIA

b) **PLAN MULTIPLE POSTS AT A TIME.** Unless you want to, there's no need to work post-by-post – why not aim to create a month's worth of social media content at a time, when your creative juices are flowing? This also gives you the chance to carefully spell-check everything ahead of time.

c) **PAY ATTENTION TO FREQUENCY.** How often should you post? It really is up to you. Whatever you decide about your posting frequency, just do your best to be consistent. When you show up regularly, people notice that.

d) **GET CLEAR ON SOMEONE FROM YOUR AUDIENCE.** Pick someone you really like from your real (or imaginary) audience, and pretend you're talking directly to them. That will help you naturally and easily project professionalism and friendliness to those you want to attract.

e) **IN GENERAL, BE CONCISE.** Science tells us that short is sweet. For example, the sweet spot for Facebook posts is 40 characters (with spaces) or less. For Instagram, research shows that "138–150 characters" is the way to go.

f) **RELATIONSHIPS ARE EVERYTHING.** What is the point of social media, if not to connect meaningfully with people? Don't forget to recognize and show enthusiasm for those who take time from their busy day to engage with your content.

g) **ASK A FEW FRIENDS AND PEOPLE FROM YOUR BOOK LAUNCH SUPPORT TEAM TO REGULARLY "LIKE" AND "COMMENT" ON YOUR POSTS.** This can give your posts a greater momentum over time, including older posts that can get "bumped up."

SOCIAL MEDIA POST IDEAS FOR AUTHORS

1. POST LINKS TO YOUR BLOG POSTS WITH AN IMAGE CONTAINING A QUOTE FROM THE BLOG
If you have an author website/blog, this type of post will bring traffic and attention to your site. Write something like this:

> [NEW BLOG POST] "Voice Acting: Get the Gear you Need to Record Professional Voice Overs from Home"
>
> Click here to read the post! [Link here]

This idea is better for Facebook than Instagram where hyperlinks aren't "live" in posts (although you can always change the links in your Instagram bio).

2. ASK FOR INPUT!
People really love to be asked for their opinions. This makes people feel good and builds excitement for an upcoming launch. As mentioned previously, people love to be asked questions about design – you will be amazed! Make sure to phrase your post as a question, e.g.,: "Which book cover design do you prefer, and why?"

3. ASK FOR HELP
Very similar to the "Ask for Input" (above) is to ask for help. So if you need help, ask! For example, if you have a question about grammar or something related to your writing. Or a productivity question. People really perk up and respond when they are asked for help.

NOTES:

GENERATING EXCITEMENT: YOUR PRE-LAUNCH CAMPAIGN, CONT.

SOCIAL MEDIA

4. ASK OTHER ENGAGING QUESTIONS RELATED TO YOUR SUBJECT MATTER

Did I say this already? People love to be asked questions. But not just any questions.

OPINIONS: As mentioned, ask people for their opinion about something (e.g., "What do you think about…?" "What would you do…?" "Which is your favorite…?" "Would you rather…?").

TRIVIA! Set up a regular (e.g., weekly) trivia post where you tickle people's brains about your topics, and let people show off what they already know!

TIP: Set a timer for 45 minutes, and type out as many interesting questions as you can think of.

5. SHOW OFF A PHOTO OF YOUR WORK AREA

For an easy behind-the-scenes post, show people a picture of where the magic happens! **BONUS**: spend a satisfying half hour cleaning and tidying your work area and putting flowers or a plant close by before staging a photo shoot.

6. TAG + THANK YOU POST!

I love thanking people (and the power of gratitude, generally). Tag and thank people for all kinds of fun and exciting reasons like helping you reach important milestones, inspiring you, for writing you a book review, or any reason at all you can think of!

Done sincerely, adding a thank you into your regular social media rotation is a beautiful and effortless way to draw people into your online social life.

7. BOOK BLURB

If you have some book endorsements/reviews, copy and paste one into a post, and find a way to turn it into a question. Of course, if you don't have any endorsements yet, please put this on your to-do list (see page 43). Make sure to tag/thank the person who wrote it for you.

8. RECYCLE SOMEONE'S COMMENT INTO A NEW POST

If someone posts a great comment or question on your page, find a way to turn it into a post to potentially start a new discussion.

9. SHARE THE AMAZING WORK OF OTHER AUTHORS

Helping incredible authors in your field, or people whose work is "peripheral" to yours, is so much fun. This is an easy post that feels good.

When done freely and regularly, the benefits can be huge. Take this a step further and reach out to the person you're admiring (e.g., by tagging them, or finding them on LinkedIn) to let them know what you love about their work, and that you're sharing it (and where)! I guarantee that it will make their day. You are putting yourself on their radar in a positive way.

10. RANDOM PAGE FROM YOUR BOOK POST

Randomly choose a page number from your upcoming book and post a mysterious screenshot of that page or a photo of your hand holding your book, if you have a printed copy. Easy and fun.

10. ENGAGING WITH PEOPLE IN GROUPS

Starting a Facebook group based around your book subject is a highly effective way to build an audience. Whenever someone joins, greet and welcome them!

NOTES:

GENERATING EXCITEMENT: YOUR PRE-LAUNCH CAMPAIGN, CONT.

SOCIAL MEDIA

A personal welcome can really have an impact on someone who is interested in you and your work, and gives you an opportunity to connect with them personally. This starts slowly, but eventually it can grow!

11. STORY POST

Although many of your posts will be short and concise (see above), people love stories: experiment with writing longer posts that tell an intriguing story, e.g., about the "why" behind your book.

> Example: [INTRO] "X years ago when I was just starting out in voice acting and I had no idea how much I had yet to learn..." [MIDDLE] "I resourcefully created a home recording studio in my basement, not realizing..." [CONCLUSION] "And now I know better! What mistakes have you made with recording? [CALL TO ACTION (optional)]. If you want to learn how to avoid the most common voice recording mistakes at home, you will love my book.

GOAL: Get people interested in you and your book in an engaging way. People love stories.

BONUS: Make it about a time you really screwed up! People will fall in love with you when you make yourself vulnerable, and it shows how confident you really are now. How did you overcome the problem?

POST IMAGE IDEAS: Post a dorky picture of you when you were younger. People love to see faces, and people love authenticity, period.

CALL TO ACTION: Ask people to tell you about something specific from their own experience.

12. CREATE A SURVEY RELATED TO YOUR SUBJECT MATTER

I am a sucker for fun surveys, and so are many others! This is quite a bit of work, but it can be a really fun way of reminding people about your upcoming book without being too overt.

FINAL TIP

Once you get going with some of these ideas, you'll find ones that you especially like, and that your audience responds to particularly well.

Make it easy for yourself, and use some of those particular types of posts over and over.

For example, if you find that people really respond to the story post, then build it into your social media and make a point to do it on a regular rotation. If everyone loves the trivia posts, do them every week or month.

If you like, you can join my growing group for writers who are in the process of becoming authors and learning to promote their book. This is a safe place to experiment with what works when it comes to promoting your book. By joining, you'll get ideas, support, and kindness.

HTTP://BITLY.COM/WRITERTOAUTHOR

CONCLUSION

In keeping with who you are, don't be afraid to be a bit wacky! A very good friend of mine (Lili!) gave me this amazing piece of business advice when I was launching my first business: don't be boring. Above all, have fun with it!

These tips can get you going when you're not sure how to engage with and build your community.

NOTES:

ORDERING PRINTED BOOKS

How can you get printed books in your hands? Here are some options.

PAPERBACK BOOKS FROM KDP

1) ORDER A **PRINTED PROOF** FROM KDP (BEFORE PUBLISHING)

If you're using Amazon KDP as a self-publishing platform, you can upload your paperback files, and then order what are called printed proofs. A proof is simply a hard copy (paper copy) of the book for you to review. *These proofs have the words "not for resale" printed across the front.*

2) ORDER **AUTHOR COPIES** FROM KDP (AFTER PUBLISHING)

If you're using Amazon KDP as a self-publishing platform, you can upload your paperback files, hit the "publish" button, wait for your book to be reviewed, and then order what are called "author copies."

Author copies are copies of your book sold to you at a low price per book (close to the cost of printing). You can buy as many as you want (in orders of up to 999 books). Essentially, you're ordering copies of your book at a wholesale rate.

The downside to ordering author copies comes when you don't live in the United States: in my experience, the books can take weeks to arrive.

PAPERBACK OR HARD COVER BOOKS FROM INGRAMSPARK

If you upload your book to IngramSpark, you have the option to print books both before making your book "live" (without distribution) and after.

DO A SHORT PRINT RUN WITH A PRINT VENDOR

Of course, there are countless print vendors who can print and bind books for you. Search for "book printing in [your area]" or ask for recommendations in any of the self-publishing Facebook groups. If you can find a local printer, you may save some money on shipping.

PRINT-ON-DEMAND (POD)

As we've discussed, POD is a wonderful innovation that allows small orders of books, (sometimes as low as one book) for a reasonable price per book.

Try **48HOURBOOKS.COM** – I have heard good things about this company.

OFFSET LITHOGRAPHY – EITHER IN YOUR HOME COUNTRY OR PRINTED IN AND SHIPPED FROM CHINA

For higher-quality books and a lower per unit price per book, you could choose to print books with an offset printer. The minimum order will be 500 or 1000, so the upfront costs to you will be higher. And you risk ending up with boxes of books in your basement. From my experience, this is only worth it if you are experienced in book sales and know ahead of time how you will distribute all these books.

NOTES:

ORDERING PRINTED BOOKS, CONT.

BOOK SPECS

In order to get a quote from a print vendor, you'll need to provide them with your book "specifications." These details include:

- Page count
- Dimensions of the book
- How many copies of the book you want
- Ink: black or full colour
- Paperback or hardcover
- Shipping info

Another specification you may want to discuss with the company's print rep is the book's paper stock (both for cover and interior). They will guide you easily through this decision.

When you request a quote, you can (optionally) ask:

- How much it will cost to get a book dummy (unprinted sample) of the book?
- How much will it cost to get a printed proof?
- How long will it take to get the shipment of printed books?

NOTES:

NOTES:

BOOK SALES AND MARKETING
MAKE A PLAN!

Recap: *selling books is harder than people expect.* Unfortunately, making a book *available* for sale isn't usually enough to sell books. More is required.

In order to sell books, you'll need to take full responsibility for selling books. That includes: a) investing in learning the skills required b) hiring people who can help you c) getting creative and/or d) all of the above. Just like with writing the book, finding ways to get it in front of readers is creative work, which gets messy at times, and almost certainly uncomfortable. Don't let that stop you.

Marketing connects your book with people who will benefit from it, helping them become aware of it. In that spirit, book marketing is an important service.

REVISIT: WHO ARE MY READERS?
Please revisit the work you did on page 63 about who your readers are. They should be at the top of your mind at all times when you're working on your book marketing plan. If your audience is Youth LGBTQQIP2SAA then you'll want to get yourself on TikTok rather than Facebook.

2-STEP ACTION PLAN: START SWIFTLY AND JOYFULLY
Here are 2 tiny baby steps you can do right now to help you get into the right mindset to sell your books. These actions are like seeds, and they will start working for you now – no matter where you are in the writing process.

ACTION 1) Make a folder on your computer called BOOK_MARKETING_PLAN

ACTION 2) Inside that, create a document and call it: DELIGHTFUL_IDEAS

** *Do this now please!*** *(waiting...)*

Every time you think of an idea that could potentially help you get your book in front of your readers, put it on the list.

But here's the secret: only put ideas on your list **THAT FEEL DELIGHTFUL!** Everyone's list will be different. Don't avoid taking any particular action just because it's outside of your comfort zone, but don't stress yourself TOO MUCH! Be a good friend to yourself.

MINDSET & ENERGY
I believe that how you feel about your book is a significant factor to sales. Whether you feel ambivalent about promoting your book (as I was with my first book) or excited, that will affect your sales. Either way, trust yourself and have some fun with this. My hope is that some of the activities in this workbook will help you better appreciate the value and beauty of your own book. Your confidence will grow. If you haven't already, please create an encouraging statement for yourself (see page 7). As sappy as this may sound, you can take the time to fall in love with your own book. And don't worry that it isn't perfect (no book ever is!).

GET READY TO LEARN!
Entire books are written about the marketing tactics below. Don't try to do them all! Instead, try to master one or two that you enjoy.

WRITE ANOTHER BOOK
This is a common piece of book marketing advice for a reason: the more books you have published, the easier it is for someone to find your other books. And, each time you write and launch a book, you'll learn more.

LEARN YOUR CHOSEN PLATFORM
This may sound obvious, but each of the major self-publishing platforms have nuances, quirks,

NOTES:

BOOK SALES AND MARKETING CONT.

strengths, weaknesses, and a learning curve. Each one provides opportunities to make your book more "discoverable" to readers. Each one is different. Whatever platform you've chosen, you'll want to spend some time getting comfortable there. Be patient. Seek out other authors who have done the same and learn from them. Watch videos.

DIGITAL MARKETING
Digital marketing means any book promotion you undertake online to encourage sales and build your audience.

AUTHOR WEBSITE, WITH HELPFUL CONTENT
If you do not have a website, don't let that stop you from moving ahead with your book's marketing plan (it's not required). However, if you do have a website (or want to create one), focus on establishing trust and rapport, and providing content that is extremely helpful to your particular audience. Dedicate at least one page (perhaps your homepage) to showcasing your book. Creating a website is beyond the scope of this workbook, but with so many web platforms available, there's never been a better time for an author to do this. However, there's also never been more competition for website traffic. Selling books directly from your website will allow you to earn more per book. However, unless you have an extremely popular website, you may not have enough traffic to sell many books. In this case, you may be better off either selling from the major self-publishing platforms, or creating a book sales funnel (below).

BOOK SALES FUNNEL
Have you ever clicked on the "Learn More" button of a Facebook ad, ended up on a landing page (a special kind of web page designed to focus your attention), and then bought something or signed up for a free PDF? This entire process is called an online sales funnel, and it is appealing because it works while you sleep. A book funnel is an online sales funnel specifically designed to help you with your book marketing goals. "Funnel-building" (as it's called) is a highly competitive and ever-evolving aspect of digital marketing with the potential to leverage your book sales, sell other digital products, and potentially bring in new clients. Due to the specialized skills required to set this up (e.g., direct sales copywriting and digital ad creation), a book funnel requires a significant investment. Since it also involves online advertising (see below), you'll need to factor in extra costs to test and tweak the ads.

ONLINE ADVERTISING
Selling products via online ads (e.g., FB, Google, Amazon AMS, BookBub, etc.) requires specialized skills, which you may be interested in learning.

However, it can also be as simple as a quick "boost" to your most popular FB posts. If you are interested in marketing your book using digital advertising, you will either have to a) learn it yourself (there are plenty of courses online, e.g., Udemy.com), or b) hire someone. Again, you'll need to allocate some of your budget to test and tweak ads in the beginning, to find out what works with your audience.

EMAIL MARKETING
Authors are often encouraged to start a newsletter. See page 51 for more information on this. People have generally become wary of giving over their emails unless they have a great reason, so you will need to find a way to motivate people to join.

SOCIAL MEDIA MARKETING
See page 69 for specific social media marketing ideas for authors. Social media marketing doesn't usually sell books directly (although there are

NOTES:

BOOK SALES AND MARKETING CONT.

exceptions). However, it's a free, fun way to connect with readers and share your professional work in a social setting.

GIVEAWAY
Almost everyone loves to win! Give away some printed copies of your book(s) and/or other enticing prizes before, during or after your launch, according to the guidelines of the platform you're using.

CONTACT BLOGGERS AND INFLUENCERS
Brainstorm a list of bloggers and influencers, who may be interested in your book. Connect with them authentically. Research what they are doing and put yourself in their shoes. Think about what they are trying to accomplish online, and see if you can help them. For example, find out if any of the bloggers on your list are open to letting you "guest blog" (writing a high-quality, unique post for their blog). Brainstorm blog post topics/headlines that are tailored to their audience. Send them a printed copy of your book. This can bring you and your work online exposure.

A BLOG TOUR: If you can find a handful of blogs on which to guest post during your book launch week, you can call it a "blog tour." Since the blog content you write for each blog needs to be unique, this requires considerable advance planning, ideally resulting in significant online exposure for your book.

MAKE A BOOK TRAILER VIDEO
Creating a trailer video for your book can be a fun way to promote your work. To do this, choose an online video-making tool such as Animoto.

AUTHOR PROFILES
To make yourself more discoverable online, sign up for free author profile pages. These are free ways to help put your book in front of readers.

☐ AMAZON AUTHOR CENTRAL
HTTPS://AUTHOR.AMAZON.COM

☐ GOODREADS AUTHOR PROGRAM
HTTPS://WWW.GOODREADS.COM/AUTHOR/PROGRAM

☐ BOOKBUB
HTTPS://INSIGHTS.BOOKBUB.COM/CATEGORY/AUTHOR-PROFILES

PUBLIC RELATIONS
It's entirely possible that a newspaper will want to write a story about what you're doing. Research online "how to write a book press release" and find some examples of book press releases to emulate. Getting media attention takes skill and effort, but it's not always as difficult as people imagine! Research and reach out to suitable journalists personally by email. Send them the link to the press release, rather than an attachment. Put as much thought as possible into writing this "pitch" email to make it compelling and concise as possible, to grab their attention.

MAKE A PRESS KIT
For authors, a press or media kit is a marketing tool that includes (but is not limited to): your book press release (see above), a high resolution headshot, an image of your book cover, endorsements, a summary of your book, your author bio and contact information. The simplest way to set this up is to post it all on a webpage.

SPEAKING

PODCASTS
If you love to talk, speaking as a guest on podcasts is a great way to showcase your expertise and bring attention to your book. Search for "podcasts about

NOTES:

BOOK SALES AND MARKETING CONT.

[your niche]" and reach out to the host with a compelling "pitch" about how you can bring value to their audience.

PUBLIC SPEAKING
If you are already a public speaker, you will want to take advantage of the opportunity to sell your books at live events.

THINKING OUTSIDE THE BOX
Recently I heard a story about an author who sneaks into bookstores and places copies of his book on bookstore shelves. He does this in the hopes that the bookstore staff will get confused during check-out, and order his book into the bookstore! This is definitely out-of-the-box thinking for an author who is getting his book "out there" with creativity.

FIND A SPONSOR
Do you know of any companies which might be suitable to sponsor your book? For example, if your book is about perfecting your tennis game, maybe there's a company who would happily give you money, pay for the printing, or give you some products in exchange for having their logo on your back cover (for example).

BOOKSTORE TOUR
One of my clients is currently contacting bookstores in various states in order to go on tour with her book. She is using IngramSpark (see more below) as her distributor for printed books. If there is demand for her book at a bookstore or library (e.g., people are specifically requesting her book), it can be ordered (print-on-demand) through IngramSpark.

PRINT BOOK DISTRIBUTION THROUGH INGRAMSPARK
Uploading your paperback files to IngramSpark costs $49. Sometimes there's a promo code available that allows you to do this for free. Once your files are reviewed and accepted, and you've enabled "Expanded Distribution," your book can be purchased through the websites of many bookstores (e.g., Barnes & Nobles), and print books can potentially be ordered in (if there's demand). For print books to be potentially ordered into a bookstore (which is rare for a self-published book), in IngramSpark your book must a) be available at the significant wholesale discount that retailers expect (between 30%–55%) and b) unsold books must be returnable (which can actually cost you money–unfortunately, authors are responsible for the costs of unsold books that are returned).

TIP: Make sure your book is priced high enough to accommodate the wholesale discount.

DISTRIBUTE "WIDE"
Going "wide" simply means offering your book for sale on multiple platforms in order to reach more readers. In contrast, self-publishers often keep their focus on Amazon KDP (the dominant bookseller).

With ebooks, you can use an ebook aggregator (e.g., Draft2Digital or Smashwords) to sell your ebook to all (or some) of the various ebook platforms (e.g., Apple, Kobo, etc.), and/or distribute your ebooks directly to those platforms.

For your print books (as mentioned), upload to IngramSpark in order to take advantage of their global distribution network.

PRE-ORDER CAMPAIGN
Also known as "pre-sales," when you set your publish date into the future and upload your book to KDP or IngramSpark, people can pre-order it. On KDP, you can set your ebook (but not paperback) for pre-order, which allows you to fine-tune your keywords etc. and set up your Author Central

NOTES:

BOOK SALES AND MARKETING CONT.

account (see page 85) before the book is published. Make sure your final file is uploaded at least 3 days in advance so that your buyers receive the correct book file.

IngramSpark allows you to pre-sell your hardcover and paperback books by setting the dates (both the publication and on-sale date) in the future during title setup. IngramSpark starts printing and shipping pre-orders about 10 days before the publish date, so make sure your final files are uploaded by then. **TIP:** Leave at least a week for the book file review process.

ASK YOUR TEAM TO SPREAD THE WORD
Ask your Book Launch Support Team (see page 25) for help spreading the word about your book! Everyone in your group signed up to help you, so be specific in your requests and don't be shy to ask for help! And ask all your friends and other random supporters (of course).

SEEK SUPPORT
When you search, you will find many incredible online resources to get book marketing ideas and support for your book marketing efforts.

FACEBOOK GROUPS
I mention Facebook groups throughout this workbook because they are a free and incredibly valuable way to find other people with shared values, interests, and knowledge.

If you like, you can join my small but growing group for writers who are in the process of becoming authors and learning to promote their books. This is a safe place to experiment with what works when it comes to promoting your book. By joining, you'll get ideas, support and kindness.

HTTP://BITLY.COM/WRITERTOAUTHOR

NOTES:

IS MY BOOK READY FOR PUBLISHING? CHECKLIST

At this point, you have likely survived a rigorous, intensive, expensive book writing and production process including developmental editing, copyediting, titling, and cover/interior book design.

If your book is starting to feel like the most shiny, beautiful, ideal version of what it can be, congratulations!

HIGH STANDARDS

If you would like strangers to reach for and buy your book, you already know that it must meet a certain minimum "adequate" (or higher) level of standard. Consumers today have sophisticated visual tastes. Without necessarily understanding why, most people can quickly recognize substandard design.

YOUR BOOK COVER

If your book cover is a DIY-type effort, as many self-published book covers are, you are to be applauded for your resourcefulness. However, your book may inadvertently show signals of "amateurism," which will create friction for your sales.

There are an incredible number of books being released on Amazon (and other book vendors) every single day. Most of them look so amateurish that no one will ever buy them. I encourage you to consider slowing down at this stage and taking the time to polish your book. You'll never regret making sure your book is the best it can be. Your book deserves that.

- [ ] **TITLE:** Compelling title/subtitle that evokes curiosity and helps orient the reader

- [ ] **ORGANIZATION:** Clear, well-organized and structured content

- [ ] **GRAMMAR AND SPELLING:** Checked and checked again after formatting

- [ ] **COVER:** The cover conveys credibility and orients the reader by being "on-genre"

- [ ] **BACK COVER BLURB IS PERSUASIVE:** Hire a copywriter or search "how to write a nonfiction book's back cover description." This is marketing copy.

- [ ] **OUTSIDE INPUT:** E.g., beta readers, advance review blurbs

- [ ] **ISBN:** One ISBN for each format (e.g., paperback, ebook, hardcover, audiobook). In the United States, purchased through Bowker for a fee. In Canada, ISBNs are free and easily accessible for self-publishers through Library and Archives Canada

- [ ] **MARKETING PLAN:** See page 81

- [ ] ....

HITTING "PUBLISH"

YAY FOR YOU!

The time has come to make your book available for sale. All your hard work has culminated in this moment.

HITTING PUBLISH

If you are using one of the self-publishing platforms, here are some of the things you need to have prepared before you can hit the "publish" button to make your book live:

METADATA

☐ **BOOK TITLE/SUBTITLE:** Make sure to input the book title *exactly* the way you did it when you registered your ISBN, with the title in the "title" field, and the subtitle in the "subtitle" field.

☐ **IMPRINT/PUBLISHER:** Double check the publisher name you used when you registered your ISBN. *That must match here,* or you could get an error. Many authors just use their name.

☐ **ISBN:** (see page 37)

☐ **YOUR BOOK DESCRIPTION:** This is sales copy for your book listing. For KDP and IngramSpark, it can be specially formatted with HTML tags. Many authors use the back cover description of the print book here (see page 51). This can be a key factor in encouraging people to buy your book.

☐ **CATEGORIES:** You'll be asked to choose a few main BISAC categories for your book (see page 39).

☐ **KEYWORDS:** Keyword phrases help make your book more discoverable. Spend some time imagining what your reader would type into the search if they were looking for a book like yours. To make the job simpler, ask your book designer if they have software that can help you with this. This can also be done manually with some research, e.g., using Google Keyword Planner and the Amazon search bar.

☐ **BOOK SPECIFICATIONS:** E.g., book dimensions, whether the interior file has a "bleed" (bleed is a print term that means the ink going to the very edge of the page), cream or white paper, etc.

UPLOAD FILES

☐ **COVER FILE:** This needs to be properly formatted to meet the platform's specifications.

☐ **INTERIOR BOOK FILE:** This needs to be properly formatted for the platform's specifications.

PRICING

☐ **PRIMARY MARKETPLACE:** If you are American, your primary marketplace will be ".com." If you are Canadian, the primary marketplace for your book will likely be ".ca."

☐ **BOOK PRICE(S):** The amount you actually earn from your self-publishing platform will be a percentage (royalty rate) of your listed book price, minus the amount it cost to produce (e.g, print) the book. At this point, you'll be able to tweak your book prices for other currencies.

AFTER YOU HIT THE "PUBLISH" BUTTON

Next comes a review period where your files are checked over for approval. If all goes well, your book will be live (available for sale) within a few days.

Congratulations, and good luck with all your book promotions (see page 81)!

NOTES:

PLANNING TOOLS

YEAR:

JANUARY	FEBRUARY
MARCH	APRIL
MAY	JUNE
JULY	AUGUST
SEPTEMBER	OCTOBER
NOVEMBER	DECEMBER

MONDAY	TUESDAY	WEDNESDAY	THURSDAY
....	....	....	....
....	....	....	....
....	....	....	....
....	....	....	....
....	....	....	....

MONTH:

FRIDAY	SATURDAY	SUNDAY	TO-DOS & NOTES
....	....	....	
....	....	....	
....	....	....	
....	....	....	
....	....	....	

MONDAY	TUESDAY	WEDNESDAY	THURSDAY
....	....	....	....
....	....	....	....
....	....	....	....
....	....	....	....
....	....	....	....

MONTH:

FRIDAY	SATURDAY	SUNDAY	TO-DOS & NOTES
....	....	....	
....	....	....	
....	....	....	
....	....	....	
....	....	....	

MONDAY	TUESDAY	WEDNESDAY	THURSDAY
…………	…………	…………	…………
…………	…………	…………	…………
…………	…………	…………	…………
…………	…………	…………	…………
…………	…………	…………	…………

MONTH:

FRIDAY	SATURDAY	SUNDAY	TO-DOS & NOTES
....	....	....	
....	....	....	
....	....	....	
....	....	....	
....	....	....	

MONDAY	TUESDAY	WEDNESDAY	THURSDAY
....	....	....	....
....	....	....	....
....	....	....	....
....	....	....	....
....	....	....	....

MONTH:

FRIDAY	SATURDAY	SUNDAY	TO-DOS & NOTES
....	....	....	
....	....	....	
....	....	....	
....	....	....	
....	....	....	

MONDAY	TUESDAY	WEDNESDAY	THURSDAY
………………	………………	………………	………………
………………	………………	………………	………………
………………	………………	………………	………………
………………	………………	………………	………………
………………	………………	………………	………………

MONTH:

FRIDAY	SATURDAY	SUNDAY	TO-DOS & NOTES
....	....	....	
....	....	....	
....	....	....	
....	....	....	
....	....	....	

SWIPE FILE

Known as a "swipe file," all copywriters keep collections of writing examples for inspiration.

If you are going to write "copy" for your book marketing efforts (e.g., website copy, the back cover of the book), welcome to the world of copywriting!

On "Activity 1: Book Title Research" on page 12, you started your own swipe file of nonfiction book titles that caught your eye. Here is space to write down more inspiring examples of writing.

YOUR PASSWORDS

Self-publishing often involves an incredible number of accounts, e.g., KDP, Amazon Author Central, IngramSpark, GoodReads, etc. Here is a handy, safe place to keep track of all your account information.

Site name:

Username: Password:

Site name:

Username: Password:

Site name:

Username: Password:

Site name:

Username: Password:

Site name:

Username: Password:

Site name:

Username: Password:

Site name:

Username: Password:

NOTES:

EDITORS AND BOOK COACHES

Editing is a key part of the book publishing process.

Here are some editors and book coaches I know, like and trust, in alphabetical order.

Each of these freelance professionals have distinct strengths, offering their own unique mix of (different types of) editing and/or book coaching.

- Stanley Dankoski, STANLEYDANKOSKI.COM
- Sigrid Macdonald, BOOKMAGIC.CA
- Nancee-Laetitia Marin, THELANGUAGEAGENT.COM
- Danielle Perlin-Good, DANIELLEPERLINGOOD.COM
- Diane Riis, WWW.EARTHANDSOULPUBLISHING.COM
- Matt Rudnitsky, WWW.RUDBITS.COM/PLATYPUS
- Jenny Watz, WRITEAMBITIONS.COM

BOOK LAUNCH SUPPORT

- Morgan Barse: WWW.WINGWOMANBRANDS.COM

OTHER HELPERS:

NOTES:

ACKNOWLEDGMENTS

Thank you to the generosity of countless incredible people who helped me with this book!

From the bottom of my heart, thank you to all my book design clients – past, present, and future! Maisha. Jenny. Lindsey. Shirley. Grace. Emma. Nicky. John. Julie. Danielle. Gaëtan. Stanley. JP. Jody. Mitch. Marie. Dan. Al. Stacie. *Thank you for working with me to transform your manuscript into an incredible book!*

Thank you to Jenny Watz for copyediting.

Thank you to my beta readers, Ashish Arya, Danielle McQuillen and Lunyz Lopez Noda from the Beta Readers and Critiques Facebook group. Thanks to readers Peggy Nehmen and Sally Jane Smith for going above and beyond.

Thank you to my wise and supportive friends Lili Wexu, Kayla Gowdy and Jason Gravel. Thank you to Velvet for always sharing your honest opinions. Thank you to Gerda Wirick for being supportive and for proofreading.

Thank you to all my friends for providing random helpful input!

Thank you to my teachers, mentors, and coaches including, but not limited to: Mike Shreeve, Delicia, Deb, Jessica, Pete, Troy, and everyone in the Peaceful Profits community.

Thank you to Nate Terrell and Mia for reminding me over and over about self-compassion.

Thanks to Ray Brehm for patiently answering my questions and helping me learn more.

Thank you to Jayme Krepps for helping me actually finish this project. Your kindness and generous guidance are so appreciated!

ABOUT THE AUTHOR

Andrea Schmidt is a freelance book designer and author who loves coffee and exclamation marks. One of her delightful design pieces was featured in HOW design magazine. She lives in Ontario, Canada. She enjoys baking bread, going to the library, and playing disc golf in the woods.

Visit Andrea online: A-SCHMIDT.COM.

CHECK OUT ANDREA'S OTHER BOOKS!

The Fun of Baking Bread: Impress Your Guests, Teach Your Kids and Never Buy Bagged Bread Again!
THEFUNOFBAKINGBREAD.COM

Mom's Christmas Planner
CANADA: www.amazon.ca/dp/099200814X | USA: www.amazon.com/dp/099200814X

Glue a picture of yourself here, smiling, and holding a book that is **YOURS**.
You wrote it, produced it, printed it and now it's in your hands.

Your book is now also in the hands of others who are enjoying and benefiting from it!
Let this picture be a commitment to **YOU**.

www.ingramcontent.com/pod-product-compliance
Lightning Source LLC
Chambersburg PA
CBHW081310070526
44578CB00006B/831